AMZ #1 BESTSELLER*

THE OFFICE DESIGN TRAP

From Cost Center to Growth Driver - The Secret Formula to Turn Your Work space into PROFIT, PRESTIGE & PERFORMANCE

AMZ #1 BESTSELLER*

THE OFFICE DESIGN TRAP

From Cost Center to Growth Driver - The Secret Formula to Turn Your Work space into PROFIT, PRESTIGE & PERFORMANCE

Ar. Pankaj Lad

Available on amazonkindle

Worldwide Published by

Pendown Press
PREMIUM BUSINESS PUBLISHER

PENDOWN PRESS LLP
An ISO 9001 & ISO 14001 Certified Co.,
Regd. Office: 3767A, Kanhaiya Nagar,
Tri Nagar, Delhi-110035
Ph.: 8130886000, 9650072927
E-mail: info@pendownpress.com
Branch Office: 1A/2A, 20, Hari Sadan, Ansari Road,
Daryaganj, New Delhi-110002
Ph.: 011-45794768
Website: PendownPress.com

Edition: 2025
Price: ₹ 399
ISBN: 978-93-7217-046-7

Layout and Cover Designed by Pendown Graphics Team
Printed and Bound in India by Thomson Press India Ltd.

Contents

Acknowledgements

First and foremost, I bow with gratitude to my parents, whose love, guidance, and blessings have been the foundation of every step I have taken in life.

To my better half, not just my better half, but truly my best half, my wife, Architect Namrata: thank you for being my pillar of strength. Your unwavering support, patience, and acceptance of who I am have allowed me to live authentically. Because you let me be myself, I've learned to give the same freedom to others, a gift beyond measure.

I am deeply thankful to my children, Aaryan and Sara, who bring light, inspiration, and joy to my journey.

My heartfelt thanks also extend to my relatives, friends, and my wonderful team @ Sarayan Architects. You have been my constant source of motivation, encouragement, and companionship. Your efforts mean more to me than words can express.

Not to forget my publisher, Mr. Dinesh Verma, CEO of Pendown Press, and his wonderful team for their valuable support in making this publishing journey smooth and joyful.

Lastly, to my dear clients, you have been an inspiration and a guiding force throughout my journey.

To my colleagues, friends, and everyone who has walked beside me, thank you for your unwavering encouragement, faith, and good wishes. Each of you has left an indelible mark on this journey, and for that, I remain forever grateful.

Preface:
The Hidden Cost of Bad Office Design

Most people feel that office design is just about choosing the right desk, stylish colors, or where to place plants. But here is the reality - this is much more than that.

What if I told you that most office spaces are failing - not due to bad coffee or old software, but because their design actively works against people inside them?

This is correct. Your office can quietly sabotage your team's productivity, your company's reputation, and even ROI.

An office blueprint is not just a background - it is a tactical tool as it shapes how people think, feel, work, and connect. It can either attract clients or push them away. This can simultaneously also activate your employees or reduce their desire to work. In a world where first impressions and daily experiences matter more than ever, poor office design can no longer tolerate a hidden cost to business.

This book reveals how companies make subtle but harmful mistakes while designing their spaces - and more importantly, how to fix them. Whether you are starting from scratch or rebuilding your current setup, you will know how to create a space that tells your brand story, fuels cooperation, and leaves every stakeholder saying: "**This is where I want to be.**"

This book reveals how companies make subtle but harmful mistakes while designing their spaces - and more importantly, how to fix them.

With over 28+ years of experience meeting thousands of business owners, corporate leaders, and admin professionals, one thing has remained constant: **Monday blues** and **Friday cheers**.

Why does the end of the week bring a sense of relaxation while the beginning feels like a burden?

But what if this story were reversed?

What if your workplace were so lively, fascinating, and purpose-driven that your staff looked forward to Mondays with the same excitement that new schoolchildren experience on their first day of classes?

What if your workspace is inspired? What if the environment you built sparked discussion, encouraged collaboration, and unlocked innovation?

Imagine a team that doesn't just show up: they ideate, innovate, integrate, and inspire. A culture where politics dissolve, synergy grows, and self-driven people work together, fueled by trust and aligned vision.

Now picture this:

- 90–95% attendance,
- high energy, zero excuses.
- Employees stop complaining about health issues because wellness is built into your workplace DNA.
- Productivity isn't a goal anymore, it's a way of life.
- Your team feels like they're working from a space that's part **Google**, part **Starbucks**, and all heart.
- Your office becomes a brand in itself, a top 10 workplace in your city.

Clients walk in and feel it instantly: credibility, culture, clarity. They want to do business with you because your space reflects your values. The office is no longer just a place; it's a powerful signal to the brain. Like a mall triggers the urge to shop, or a waterpark evokes joy, your office sparks contribution, growth, and excellence.

Now imagine this—after creating such a space, your profits don't just grow... they multiply. 10x. 20x. 50x.

So, what's stopping you?

The answer is: Bad Design!

An office with outdated furnishings, neutral lighting, cluttered space, or a design that inhibits communication can have the opposite impact. It fosters dissatisfaction and boredom rather than motivation. Regardless of the scope of your vision, a poorly organized workplace makes employees feel disconnected, discouraged, and bored. The very atmosphere supposed to encourage creativity might actually hinder it. So, if design is so integral to creating the culture and productivity you dream of, why risk letting poor choices in your office space hold you back from the future you want to build?

Here's the uncomfortable truth you must know:

Every time you compromise on a key design decision, lighting, space management, collaborative spaces, ergonomics, environment, culture, you might be quietly losing **lakhs or even crores of rupees in hidden costs**, and this is what most of the businesses fail to understand.

High absenteeism. Declining morale. Unproductive meetings. Poor wellness. Missed client opportunities.

They all have one thing in common: they're rooted in the *space* you've created.

Look back at the last 1 to 3 years.

Now connect the dots.

- How much potential growth have you blocked?
- How much money has been wasted during this timeline?
- How many great people, great ideas, or great clients walked away without ever telling you why?

That's not just lost revenue:

- That's **missing momentum**.
- That's **10x potential**, unrealized.
- That's **a future you could've owned**... if your design had supported your vision.

So, ask yourself the big question:

Was it worth it? Or, are you paying the cost of BAD DESIGN?

Well, this book reveals how companies make subtle but harmful mistakes while designing their spaces - and more importantly, how to fix them. Whether you are starting from scratch or rebuilding your current setup, you will know how to create a scope that tells your brand story, fuels cooperation, and leaves every stakeholder saying:

"This is where I want to be."

Why This Book & Why Now!

"Jaisa kaam ka space, waisi team ki pace."
As the workspace is, so is the team's pace.

Now, I am sure you must be thinking, Why have I decided to write this book now? What forced me to reach out to you?

Hi, I am **Ar. Pankaj Lad,** working architect, design strategist, and your navigator onto the confusing, expensive, and often chaotic highway of workspace design.

Let me answer your unspoken question and tell you why I wrote this book, and most importantly, how and why it fits in with the current workspace scenarios across the globe.

I've spent more than two and a half decades, to be precise, 28+ years in the world of workspace design. I started my journey at **Godrej & Boyce** and eventually partnered with businesses of every shape, size, and scale: from startups and MSMEs to major corporations alike.

And there's a specific and repetitive pattern I've seen time and again, especially in India.

Office design is often treated as a numbers game.

- "How many people can we squeeze and fit into this much space?"
- "How much per sq. ft. are we spending?"

This obsession with **cost per square foot**, while understandable in expensive metros like Mumbai (where property rates shoot past Rs. 50,000 per sq. ft.), has led to a culture of **overcrowded, uninspiring, soul-crushing workplaces.**

I've seen employees packed into 2x2 ft desks in call centers.

I've seen talented people quit just because the office felt more like a prison than a place of purpose.

And I've seen business leaders genuinely wonder *why* their teams aren't motivated, productive, or loyal.

Let me ask you this:

Can a high-performing team grow in a low-performing environment?

The answer is obvious. Yet it's a blind spot for so many.

Contrast this with human-centric organizations like Apple, Google, or Amazon, whose office spaces are **designed to drive performance.**

Recreation zones, breakout areas, natural light, casual collisions, all aimed at nurturing wellness, sparking ideas, and fueling collaboration.

Steve Jobs understood this decades ago. At Pixar, he placed the washrooms and pantries centrally just so people would bump into each other and talk, because innovation, he believed, happened **between meetings, not just in them.**

Why should this level of intention be reserved for Silicon Valley giants?

Why can't Indian MSMEs, with offices as compact as 3,000 sq. ft., enjoy the same design-driven momentum?

From 100 to 250 Crores

The Transformation That Made Mondays Magical

Let me tell you about **Star Plastics,** a family-run business with a turnover of around 100 crores.

Two years ago, they worked out of a modest 1,500 sq. ft. office in an industrial area. They acquired an adjacent unit, added a mezzanine, and we had 3,000 sq. ft. to work with.

No glass towers. No sea views. Just a narrow, rectangular gala.

But what we did **within that space** changed everything.

How we created magic:

- Introduced a **breakout zone** (yes, even with limited space)
- Designed **motivational branding zones** aligned with their company values
- Added **glass partitions** on the mezzanine to pull in natural light and preserve openness
- Created a **multipurpose zone,** serving as a conference room, lunchroom, and area for collaboration.
- Added **biophilic elements** and subtle wellness cues
- Deliberately crafted a **visitor experience area** with differentiated flooring
- Carved out **workstations for visiting sales executives,** making them feel integrated, not sidelined

All within budget. No frills. Just function with finesse.

The result?

- Their revenue surged **2.5x**, now crossing around 250 crores.
- Team retention skyrocketed.
- And the workplace? It now gets a consistent "*wow*" from every visitor.

People want to come to work. Even on Mondays.

Not because of some fancy HR policy, but because the **space makes them feel seen, valued, and energized.**

The Turning Point In The Story

This transformation didn't create success from scratch, **but it amplified it**.

The business already had a strong backbone.

What the new design did was **unleash untapped potential** and **unlock a new orbit of growth.**

That's what this book is about.

- ➢ It's a wake-up call for every Indian business that's still treating office design as an afterthought.
- ➢ It's a call to action for MSMEs and corporates alike to stop squeezing productivity out of people, and start **designing it into space**.

Because your office isn't just an address.

It's your **culture in 3D.**

It's your **silent recruiter, your brand story, your innovation hub,** if you design it right.

Why This Book Matters

India's economy is on the rise. Our Honorable Prime Minister has already declared that MSMEs contribute **30%** of the nation's total revenue. But here's a bold question — why can't it be **50%**? Why can't Indian MSMEs and corporates grow exponentially and take center stage on the global map? Because if businesses grow, the country grows. And when India grows, the world watches.

We are already on the path to becoming a global economic powerhouse. But what can truly propel us faster is creating the right work environment. That is the core purpose of this book: nation-building. If I can contribute even a little toward this mission, I would consider my 28+ years of experience worthwhile.

Over these years, I've closely observed foreign companies, global MNCs, and our own Indian organizations. And I keep asking: What are these companies doing differently that we are not? India has the talent. We have the expertise. We have the ambition and drive. So what's missing?

The answer lies in one simple, but powerful concept: **Human Wellness**.

These successful companies care for their people. They focus on how people work, where they work, and how they feel while they work. They invest in ergonomics. They pay attention to the environment their employees spend time in — the air quality, the lighting, the temperature, the design, and the energy of the space. These are not small details. These are the factors that shape employee health, focus, creativity, and productivity.

In the upcoming chapters, you will discover how light impacts the brain, how inadequate air circulation causes exhaustion, and how the lack of natural components causes us to lose touch with our true selves. We are living creatures made to flourish in environments that are natural, light-filled, and peaceful; we are not machines. However, we spend 50% of our waking hours in uninspired environments, surrounded by screens and artificial light.

No wonder we see rising cases of stress, high blood pressure, anxiety, and burnout. The stress levels of the working population today are alarming — and this is not just anecdotal. According to a Harvard study, when people are placed in thoughtfully designed, wellness-driven environments that stimulate their senses and reconnect them with nature, something known as biophilia, their cognitive performance improves by **20–25%**.

So the question is: Why wait?

Why should your employees spend their days in dull, draining offices when you can design a space that energizes them, supports their well-being, and maximizes their potential?

Now is the time. Not just to improve productivity. But to build workplaces that serve as engines of national growth and pride. The wellness of your people is not a luxury; it's the basis of your company's tomorrow.

And if we can get this right, we're not just building better businesses — we're building a better India.

So let's rethink the way India works.

Let's build spaces that do more than just fit people in; let's design offices that **inspire people to grow, thrive, and stay.**

And now, I have written this book for you.

- For the **Corporates** who are tired of hearing false promises on social media and magazines.
- For the **smart MSME business owners** who are scared of hiring just another interior guy.
- For the **business leaders** who have lost money on "**cheap**" band-aid fixes that ended up really costing big down the line.
- For the **inspired one** who wants an office that works just as hard for them as they do.

This book doesn't just travel around the pretty picture scenes.

Think of it as a truth bomb in blueprint form: practical, brutal, real.

This is so because through this book, you will learn to:

- Cut **unnecessary costs** without cutting corners
- Design with **brand, function, and people in mind**
- Avoid the **top mistakes** that lead to budget blowouts
- Create **WOW-worthy spaces** without celebrity designer fees
- **Build smarter,** no matter the size of your team or budget

So, let's start the magical journey of turning your workspace into a **WOW** experience.

Chapter 1

Beyond Aesthetics
The Real Purpose of Office Design

Why Office Design is Not Just a Decoration?

> **The beauty of a workplace lies in its functionality.**
>
> *– Ar. Pankaj Lad*

Office design goes beyond just aesthetics as it contributes to the productivity of employees, followed by promoting collaboration and strengthening the brand identity of a company. A well-planned workspace can change workflow efficiency with the creation of an environment that leads to creativity and conception.

Alongside, carefully thought-out office design helps businesses in making powerful first impressions on clients and stakeholders, setting the tone for quality and prosperity. Companies can create spaces that don't just look impressive but also lead to business growth and worker contentment by balancing the function with form.

Psychological Outcomes of Space on Productivity and Optimism

The scope of a design has a powerful effect on a person's mental state, accompanied by motivation and overall productivity. Vital factors such as natural lighting, seating arrangement, color schemes, and noise levels can either increase focus and creativity or give rise to stress and chaos.

A well-structured office promotes a sense of belonging, inspiration, and efficiency by creating an environment that coincides with human psychology. For example, open spaces lead to cooperation, while designated calm areas support deep work.

In addition, elements such as ergonomic furniture, greenery, and individual spaces help in employee welfare, decrease burnout, and increase job satisfaction. Keeping psychology in mind, businesses can be a place that empowers employees and promotes the culture of innovation and success.

Common Misunderstandings About Workplace Aesthetics

Given that humans automatically associate a well-designed room with vibrant hues, elegant furniture, or premium décor, many people think that office design is all about visual appeal. However, when crafting such places, it is important to constantly keep in mind that utility and aesthetics should be coordinated. Another general myth is that open-concept offices promote cooperation; In fact, there may be distractions from poorly employed open locations and can decrease productivity.

Additionally, businesses often ignore the effects of elements such as light, sound, and ergonomics, which play an important role in creating an area that is not only visually attractive but also efficient and comfortable. True workplace aesthetics should basically integrate brand recognition, employee welfare, and operational efficiency rather than focusing on surface-level design trends.

⃠⃠⃠⃠

Chapter 2

Designing for Power and Credibility

Performance metrics and financial results aren't the only way to earn authority and credibility in the contemporary competitive business world. They are also projected, perceived, and reinforced by visual and spatial cues, **none more direct or physical than the design of a company's physical space.**

As soon as a guest enters the office, they start drawing conclusions about the company's status, what it stands for, and whether or not its legitimate office design is not just about looks. It's a strategic tool that communicates brand identity, inculcates trust, and expresses power.

The main purpose of this chapter is to explore how office environments help you generate brand authority, form first impressions within seconds, and learn things like what other companies in the Fortune 500 list have done well in customising for credibility. Just by this fact alone, you can see the importance of designing and credibility.

The Silent Language of Space: How Brand Authority Is Affected by Office Design

Design is a language: space is its most persuasive grammar. Just as we pick up someone's rank by his gestures, we judge a company's strength by the signs and symbols of elevation that are built into its physical environment: its layout, its furniture, its lighting, the materials it uses, its works of art, even the smell. Office design is a kind of brand narrative that either outstands or undermines the story you're trying to tell.

For example: A law firm with traditional dark wood paneling, framed degrees, and leather furniture shows its seriousness and has a sense of legacy. A tech startup with exposed ceilings, glass walls, and communal work spaces makes the impression of innovation and openness. However, every design option a company takes has one outcome or another, but never both.

It is vital to realize that these cues usually go on at the subconscious level. Both visitors and employees very often do not register these cues consciously, but they feel them. In a nutshell, the cues find their way even in the slightest gestures, such as the firmness of a handshake transmitted across a sleek conference table, the manner in which voices bounce around the open offices, or the muted aura of a bright, neat reception area.

First Impressions: What Your Office Tells Visitors Within the First 5 Seconds

Environmental psychology studies have found that people make lasting judgments about an unknown or unfamiliar place within seconds as soon as they enter such a space. The same goes for a person entering into the office; they do not wait for you to pitch an idea or extend a handshake to decide your credibility; rather, they look around and decide the same within a few seconds as soon as they enter the place, and some of the deciding factors are as follows:

- **The Reception Area**: This is the focal point of the so-called impression-building scenario. If it's chaotic, cluttered, or, as usual, an impression of chaos or lifelessness is created. Whereas a clean, clear, minimalist space evokes precision, attention to detail, and is very contemporary.

- **Furniture and Layout:** Ergonomic furniture stresses the fact that the employee's well-being is a priority. Custom furniture, on the other hand, that includes desks with embedded branding or interactive displays-indicates innovation and smart investment. The furniture layout is either hierarchical with large executive offices or impartial, with open desks; one way or the other, it speaks of the culture and values of the company.
- Here, one of the most vital factors to keep in mind is the environment and geography of the workspace, as that plays one of the primary roles in shaping the employees' work experience and overall wellness. Something that can work in Indian workspaces is not necessarily to fit in American workspaces due to variation in working style, and thus it is extremely vital to keep in mind the place factor while designing furniture and layout part of your workspace. Because other facts are universal, but this one varies according to geographical location.
- **Lighting and Color:** Ugly or unpleasant fluorescent lights bring with them administrative notions and dullness, whereas a symphony of natural light and warm LEDs integrates comfort and alertness. Then comes the color psychology-blue and green will work for trust and balance, respectively; contrast that with red signifying urgency or passion, and black is all about sophistication or dominance.
- **Branding Presence:** Subtle yet consistent marketing, such as a logo carved in transparent glass or trademark colors utilized in furniture and wall paintings, quickly connects the office to the company's identity. This kind of consistency and attention to detail helps a brand become trustworthy.
- **Technology and Cleanliness:** A careless environment with outdated equipment and messy cables, and corners loudly

says "**neglect**" to the visitors. Conversely, cutting-edge spaces with clean integration of technology reflect on forward thinking and innovation.

Office Design and Brand Authority

Office design is a visual metaphor representing the operational values and brand identity of a company's operational values. When done well, it impresses and changes behavior inside and outside.

- **External Authority:** An office is the first genuine interaction most clients, investors, and partners will have with your company. It is in those moments that perception becomes reality.

  A luxe setting does not simply lead to monetary success; it also implies quality, confidence, and exclusivity. An office can justify pricing, attract elite clients, and help close deals quickly. And that is exactly why luxury brands and top consultancies spend considerable amounts on their spaces.

- **Internal Authority:** A professional office design also communicates to employees. It promotes a sense of pride, enhances productivity, and promotes culture. Employees feel strong when their environment reflects purpose and success. From the open churning lounge to private pods for focused work, design options suggest that the company gives importance to both cooperation and personality.

In such environments, hierarchy and transparency can be physically mapped, clear, concise, shared locations for officials that invite cross-delivery interactions, and strengthen access to reach and alignment with zone leadership designed for informal dialogues.

Fortune 500 Companies Designing for Credibility:

Inspiring Case Studies

Let's have a glance at how the leading companies of the world are designed for power, prestige, and strategic effects.

Apple: Minimalism Meets Monumentality

Apple Park, the company's worldwide headquarters in Cupertino, is an excellent representation of the brand image. A building like a circular spaceship is not just an achievement of engineering-**it is a statement of future vision, innovation, and unique ambition.**

Inside, the design follows minimum principles - open spaces, clean lines, glass, and an abundance of natural materials. **The effect is one of cool dominance.** There is no chaos, no disorganization. Just **focus on clarity and confidence**. Visitors passing through the space feel that they are entering the future.

Apple's design options, from custom furniture to Serene Landscaping, broadcast that it is a company with resources and discipline to control every detail - an unexpected but **powerful statement of authority**.

Goldman Sachs: Tradition Reinforced with Modern Power

Goldman Sachs' offices mix traditional corporate gravity with contemporary style. Their headquarters in New York has limestone walls, a bronze finish, and rich wooden paneling, all of which provoke a **sense of stability, durability, and heritage.**

At the **same time, they include glass offices and contemporary art to indicate openness and modernity**. Higher floors are lined with the distinctive 'lunar wall,' while centrally placed offices for senior officials are designed as transparent but enclosed spaces, emphasizing hierarchy within visibility.

This amalgamation of old and new is a strategy: it appeals to long-term investors and institutions, while the youth elements are attractive to talent and startup partners. This suggests that Goldman Sachs is both contemporary and timeless.

Google: Innovation Embodied

Googleplex, especially in the complex of Google, is famous for its unconventional, playful designs. Think about a nap pod, a slide between the floor, and a themed meeting room. But this is not surface-level - it is deeply tactical.

Google is making a clear statement: we are not bound by convention by designing **offices that feel like creative playgrounds compared to rigid workplaces**.

This design promotes risks, experimentation, and cross-disciplinary cooperation, which are required for enthusiasts.

Externally, **it tells partners, users, and governments that Google is different**. Internally, it promotes the culture that has allowed the company to be ahead of the competition for decades.

Amazon: Frugality as Power

Amazon's design strategy takes the opposite direction. In its early offices, the **company's famous culture of frugality was made visible:** recycled doors served as desks, furniture was minimal, and unnecessary decorations were avoided.

Yet even this conveyed a sense of power. **It reflected focus, discipline, customer obsession, and a kind of primal clarity of thought.** This design language **emphasized that the company values performance** above all else.

As Amazon grew, its spaces became more refined, but even in its newer buildings, such as the Spheres in Seattle, there remains a deliberate rejection of excessive luxury. Instead, the design communicates practicality, purpose, and restraint."

Psychological Effects on Visitors and Staff

The design does more than the perception of size; This affects behavior. The office design can encourage design productivity, loyalty, creativity, and even moral behavior.

- **Confidence and Trust:** Visitors who walk into a thoughtfully designed office are more likely to rely on the company. **Harvard Business Review** Studies found that the physical environment directly affects the level of confidence in potential business partners. Clean lines, consistent design, and quality material give people subconscious assurance that they are in capable hands.
- **Productivity and Creativity:** The design of a space affects energy levels and cooperation. For example, Google's flexible locations encourage movement and serious interactions, promoting creativity. Whereas calm green fields and individual-focused work help to promote deep work.

- **Talent Attraction and Retention:** Top talent, especially young generations, often consider the work environment as part of their decision-making process. A powerful, well-designed space is a recruitment tool. This concludes that the company cares not only about the results, but also about the experience of the employees.

Useful Tips: Designing for Credibility at Any Scale

You do not need a **Fortune 500 budget** to design the location that communicates the authority. Let me give you a prime example of how you can fit things in the boxes without misplacing anything and getting 10/10 when it comes to your workspace design in all aspects:

Design Isn't Decoration: It's Direction

A Case Study

Mr. Bharadwaj spent **5.25 crores** on a Fancy Office Makeover, and watched his business decline by **27%**

Rajat Bharadwaj wasn't a flashy man. He ran a reputable insurance consultancy: constant clients, a reliable team, and a decade of quiet growth behind him.

But when newer companies started popping up with glass-walled offices, mood lighting, and Instagram-friendly corners, he panicked. "**Maybe we look too old-school**," he thought.

So he pulled 5.25 crores from his expansion fund and hired a trendy interior contractor.

Three months later, the office looked like any other tech startup company based in Gurugram instead of an insurance consultancy: black marble reception, LED-lit ceilings, angular furniture, and a high-gloss conference room with zero privacy.

The Result?

- Client engagement dropped by 27%.
- His longest-serving employee quietly resigned.
- And one loyal client casually asked, "Is this a showroom now?"

That's when he was referred to me by a mutual contact, with a single line: ***"Talk to Ar. Pankaj Lad. He'll tell you what's actually wrong."***

When I walked into the space, the problem hit me immediately:

The design was impressive, but completely disconnected from the business.

- It didn't say "**trust.**"
- It didn't say "**stability.**"
- It didn't say "**we've got you covered**"
- It said... "**We're trying too hard.**"

I sat down with Mr. Bharadwaj, and we reframed the entire approach, not from a place of trend, but from **truth**.

We:

- Swapped the **sterile gloss** for **matte, earthy textures**
- Introduced warm **lighting** and **natural finishes** that felt calm, not corporate
- Replaced **flashy art** with a wall that told his **company's origin story**
- Created a **soundproof client lounge** with **soft seating and subtle** cues of credibility, certificates, testimonials, and even a framed letter from his first client Repositioned the **layout** to encourage eye contact and conversation, not intimidation

Within six weeks:

- Walk-in conversion improved by **34%**
- Client feedback called the space "**inviting**," "**credible**," and "**genuine.**"
- Team morale surged, and two former employees even reconnected about rejoining

"I thought design was about looking expensive," Mr. Bharadwaj told me later. "Turns out, it's about *feeling right.* You helped me remember who we are, and made the space say it out loud."

He didn't need a flashy renovation.

- He needed a mirror that reflected his business's values, not someone else's trends.
- And when design aligns with identity, the numbers speak for themselves.

Through this example, we came across the fact of how important design is when it comes to the overall growth and smooth functioning of any workspace.

Hence, some of the key factors to keep in mind while designing your space are:

- **Audit your entry experience:** What someone sees in the first 5 seconds after entering your place, listens and feels?
- **Prefer clean lines and form:** Simplicity often feels more powerful than complexity.
- **Invest in quality materials:** Some well-chosen, high-quality pieces (a designer desk, elegant lighting, and stability) can elevate the entire room.

- **Use color strategically:** Align your color palettes that aligns with your brand and desired emotional response.
- **Include brand elements:** Logo, mission statement, and cultural artifacts help to tie the location to your company's identity.
- **Be consistent:** From the bathroom to the boardroom, every detail matters.
- **Design for your audience:** If you serve high-end customers, select the option of a luxury finish. If you are serving tech firms, go modern and agile.

Office design is one of the most underutilized elements for projecting authority and credibility of the building. This is not just a background for business - it is a statement, a message, a brand experience in three dimensions.

Whether you are running a lean startup or managing a huge multinational, your place tells a story. Ensure that it is one of strength, vision, and reliability. Because in business, perception often occurs before performance, and the correct design helps to ensure that both of them increase in the forefront.

⦸⦸⦸⦸

Chapter 3

Beyond Aesthetics

Creating an Experience, Not Just a Space

> **"People will forget what you said, people will forget what you did, but people will never forget how you made them feel."**
>
> – *Maya Angelou*

Let's straighten one thing: "**Good enough**" is not officially enough.

- Not for office design.
- Not for impression-making.
- And of course not for brands that want to lead, motivate, or interrupt.

In an era where Instagrammable Corners, TikTok Office Tours, and Google Reviews shape senses towards spaces, your office has to do more than work - it has to breathe emotions, to breathe curiosity, and spark joy.

Welcome to the era of experienced design. In this chapter, we are going to the full throttle in the world of offices that **WOW**, and let's unfold how the smallest, the smartest touch can increase your environment from passive to unforgettable.

Why "Good Enough" is Now a Dead Sentence

A. **The Curse of Vanilla:** If your office feels like a box of beige drywall, you are not just boring your employees - **you are**

sending a signal to customers and investors that your creativity, passion, and innovation are probably also flat. According to the report of the global workplace of Steelcase, **88% highly satisfied employees also report high workplace engagement,** and the space design is a major reason.

B. **Brains Love Novelty:** Our brains are hardwired to notice differences. When something stands out - an unexpected ceiling installation, an odor that reminds us of travel, or a custom soundscape - it attracts attention and emotionally anchors us into that memory. Dr. Carmine Gallow, in his book Talk to Ted, suggests that innovation brings light to the reward center of the brain - especially, the release of dopamine, which enhances memory and engagement.

What is Experimental Design, Really?

Imagine if your office was not just a desk, a collection of chairs, and strangely potted plants placed randomly, but instead a multi-sensory journey that spoke the story of your brand, reflected its culture, and went to the people, "**Wow ... that sure sounds different.**"

Experienced design is not about gimmick - it is intentional. It is the art and science of preparing emotional moments through space so that the experience of the visitor becomes the signature of your brand.

At its core, the experimental design asks three questions:

- **What should people feel here?**
- **What should they remember?**
- **What should they do next?**

Let's answer those questions.

Impressions That Stick: The Power of Moments

A. **First Impressions Are Performances:** Forget the welcome desk. Think of arrival choreography. When someone walks into your office, whatever they see, smell, listen to, and touch is a performance - and you are the director.

At the headquarters of **Airbnb**, each meeting room is built after actual Airbnb houses around the world, and each interaction has been converted into a micro-travel experience that reflects the mission of the brand, "**anywhere**".

- **Spotify's NYC office** attaches to hearing memory at the door with a curated playlist in the lobby - an immediate emotional hook that confirms their music DNA.
- ***Takeaway:*** Don't let your entrance be forgettable. Make it feel like Act I of a powerful story.

A. **Flow Isn't Just for Yoga:** Experienced design thrives on movement with intuitive knowledge. Your office should feel naval, not like a maze. The layout should guide people through moments of happiness.

   For example, **Dropbox** has designed a **"library corridor"** that flows from collaborative areas to deep-focus areas, helping employees to rebuild mentally and emotionally as they move through space.

Takeaway: Map your space like a story arc—intro, build-up, climax, reflection.

Wow Without Shouting: Subtle Touches, Massive Impact

A. **Scent: The Undercover Influencer:** Our **olfactory system** is tied directly to cognitive and emotional memory. A **2016** study in the **Journal of Environmental Psychology** found that a positive perception of **70%** increased in the smell-prosperous environment.

➢ **Strategic fragrance** - such as lavender in cool areas, citrus in creative areas, or even a custom branded mixture - can immediately grow how your location is experienced.

Takeaway: Want to be remembered? Start by tickling their noses.

B. **Art With Intention:** Use art as an emotional message as wallpaper. **Twitter's SF Office** established tweet murals to show the ingredients of user-related materials, embedded social evidence, and brand values on the walls.

➢ **The Salesforce Tower in San Francisco** showed the art installations that support the subjects of diversity and innovation, customised to reflect the developed story of the brand.

Takeaway: Art isn't wall filler. It's visual storytelling.

C. **Sound Design:** The **Acoustic Environment** shapes mood, productivity, and cooperation. Research by the **University of California, Irvine** found that inconsistent noise is more concentrated than forecasted or curated soundscapes.

➢ **Soft music** in the lounge, white noise in focus areas, and themed soundscapes in the theme rooms help place the anchor's feeling.

Takeaway: The right sounds help people shift gears, without saying a word.

Designing Your Own WOW (Without a Fortune 500 Budget)

Not every brand has a Bezos budget. Fortunately, **WOW isn't about money; it's about meaning**.

A. **Anchor to Emotion:** Choose three brand-psychological sentiments, such as confidence, creativity, or curiosity. Then design every corner to support them. **Emotional design = Memorable place**.

B. **Micro-Experiences Matter**

   Small details make large impressions:

   - Local reception snacks = authenticity
   - Guest name digital signage = privatization
   - Chalkboard Ideas Walls = engagement

C. **Curate Over Create:** You do not need to invent everything.

Curate meaningful elements:

- A "**Wall of Firsts**" (first logo, first office photo, first team)
- Founder's desk exhibition
- Timeline corridor with milestones

Takeaway: These elements are like emotional breadcrumbs - the leading visitors in your story deeply.

From Workspace to Stage

Designing an office is no longer about arranging the desk. It is about crafting the moments that transform visitors into believers and employees into evengelists.

Question yourself:

- Does your office heart beat rapidly?
- Does it whisper about your values even in silence?
- Do they reach for their phones to catch this moment?

If not, this is the time to **reconsider, reimagine,** and **re -reinstatement**. Because the future is of those who design not only for productivity, but also for appearance.

⦸⦸⦸⦸

Chapter 4

The Role of Luxury in Office Design

Walk to Cartier or any famous law firm, and before you feel, you will understand one thing: **Luxury**. But this luxury is not about chandeliers or gold-trimmed boardroom chairs. The true luxury in office design is more psychological than decorative, more about substance than the surface.

In this chapter, we talk about the real luxury in the design of the office, how to shape the perception of premium content, and how you can strike the balance between sophistication and work, without slipping into a solid oppression.

Luxury Vs. Opulence: Knowing the Difference

The Subtle Science of "Enough"

Let's start with a truth bomb: luxury is restrained, not more. Opulence shouts for attention, while luxury whispers. For example, a fine-grain walnut finish, accurately cut stone, and a well-balanced door handle weight. These are not accidents - they are intentionally designed decisions to create an **advanced sensory experience**.

Dr. Jonathan Chapman, Professor of Sustainable Design at Carnegie Mellon, says this "**Emotional Durability**" - the idea that luxury is not abundant, but comes from meaning and tact.

Take the store of Apple: Smooth, minimal, passionately clean. Luxury has not been called - it has been felt. This same philosophy applies to Apple Park's office design: curved glass, custom aluminum, and invisible seams. It's not "**Rich**," it's sophisticated.

The Psychology of Perception: Premium = Powerful

The Status Signal Effect

Luxury design is not only about materials - it is about how they affect material perception. **Researchers at the London School of Economics** found that the physical environment with a high-end effect affects the perceptions of brand prestige and reliability.

So yes, the cost of a marble reception desk may be higher, but it pays dividends in confidence. A wall clad in fluted oak or custom leather immediately triggers a brain relationship with quality, capacity, and uniqueness. Luxury communicates that you care about expansion - and if you care a lot about space, then of course you also care about your customers and products. It is a subconscious equation that occurs rapidly. In fact, according to environmental psychology studies, **first impressions of space are formed within 1/10th of a second.**

The Power of Premium Materials

Touch Is the New Trust

The material speaks before your team even gets a chance to pitch. That suede-lipped boardroom chair? It says "**Decisive but Thoughtful.**" Burned brass light stability? "**Inheritance comes from Modernity.**"

According to a study published in the **Journal of Consumer Psychology**, people are more likely to rate a company when wood or leather-like hot, touch materials, such as metal or plastic, interact with cold materials.

Let's break down some hero material in luxury design:

- **Natural Stone (e.g., travertine, marble):** Timely elegance. Indicates durability and investment.
- **Hardwoods (e.g., walnut, oak):** Hot, reliable, and universally upscale.
- **Brass & Bronze:** Classic meets contemporary. Weight and visuals add heat.
- **Textured Glass or Smoked Mirror:** The mystery and depth connect without heaviness.

Functional Sophistication: Luxury That Works

Form Meets High-Function

Luxury does not mean "**Look, don't touch**", the most elite office works with the design, with the entertaining.

At the **Paris headquarters of LVMH**, private spaces in the form of showrooms double, while a modular executive desk hides technology with spontaneous integration. Everything looks comfortable - because it is an engineer to be.

Similarly, a $1.3B workspace designed by **Bloomberg's London Office**-Foster + Partners is placed as one of the world's most durable and user-friendly buildings. Here, luxury means eco-ecclested smart tech, cool air diffuser, and curved bronze blades that react to the sun's position throughout the day.

When Luxury Goes Wrong: Design Don'ts

Overdesign = Overkill

Ever been to a place that seemed that it was more like a palace than a workplace? Excessive use of lux content without reconciliation or utility may **intimidate instead of inspire**.

Psychologist Donald Norman gave an aesthetic **usability effect** idea- people seem to judge design not only on beauty, but how easy it seems.

Very high brightness, too much texture, very little clarity = confusion, not comfort.

Achieving Sophisticated Luxury on a Budget

Smart Spending, Big Impact

Not every company can afford Calacatta marble and Philippe Starck fixtures. But luxury isn't about cost per square foot; it's about impact per square inch.

High-Return Design Moves:

- **Declaratory Piece Strategy:** Invest in one attractive piece for each space, such as a sculpted piece of furniture, an overhead light, or a wall paneled in handcrafted leather. Encourage it to uplift everything in the area around it.

- **Improve the Touchpoints:** Hardware, faucets, and handles on doors are high-touch areas that impact how well a good design is received.
- **Curated Palette:** Calm assurance is displayed by a soothing, layered color scheme that amalgamates rich accent tones (such as slate, midnight blue, or moss) with calm neutrals.
- **Framed Simplicity:** Open regions, large-format wall art, and architectural lighting can all seem more lavish than crowded décor.

Luxury is a Language

Luxury office design is not about making monuments for funds. It is about crafting the atmosphere that objects to value, trust, and timelessness through every surface, seam, and silence.

It is not about the cost - it is about care. It is not about flash - it's about feeling.

So whether you are preparing a flagship headquarters or designing a 500 square feet studio again, ask yourself:

- **Does your place reflect restraint or ego?**
- **Is your content screaming or speaking?**
- **Are people feeling reputation - or just the price?**
- Because in the world of office design, luxury is not the only thing they see - this is what they remember.

Chapter 5

The Power of Collaborative Spaces

Collaboration Isn't Just a Trend, It's Today's Competitive Advantage

> **"Architecture is designing the space as per the prevailing culture and not otherwise."**
>
> *– Ar. Pankaj Lad*

Every groundbreaking idea begins with "**What if...?**"

The magic spark of innovation often strikes in moments of shared energy, not solitary conflict. Modern businesses know this: you cannot do siloed creativity. This is so because today's agile spaces, flexible hubs, breakout nooks, open-plan benches-where strategy and serendipity collide.

In this chapter, let's unpack:

- Why do businesses live on cooperation?
- How to strike the correct balance between openness and retreat?
- And how to design the meeting room and breakout areas that set fire to efficiency and imagination.

Buckle up, as we are going to explore the advantages of collaborative spaces.

Why Modern Businesses Thrive on Collaboration

A. **Collaboration as Culture and Currency:** Think of your most powerful thoughts. Were they born in separation... or in conversation? A 2021 study on a colleague's environment found that cooperation directly promotes innovation - and often prepares the business model completely. More than just conversation, cooperation is culture. This is the place where diverse minds collide, produce friction, and then spark successes.

Surprisingly, a major environmental psychology survey found that integrating natural materials and flexible areas in offices can increase productivity - and significantly, cooperation - up to **15%**.

B. **Big Picture: Trust, Serendipity, and Speed:** Galp's "**State of the American Workplace**" reported that face-to-face conversations lead to trust faster than digital Chatter. And trust? This is the key to alignment. As the CEO of Steelcase said back in 2015, distant work is very good - until you remember the magic that is in the person. Businesses should be provided with spacious places.

Use these situations correctly, and see ideas coming to life with the right decisions.

Open-Plan vs Private: The Eternal Tension

A. **The Case for Open Plans:** Open-plan offices provide visibility, flexibility, and low cost. They look collaborative- open desks, bouncy areas, tight spaces. **According to Spacepool**, such setups help teams network, share knowledge quickly, and access as required.

Statistically:

- **47%** more profit for communication-rich layouts.
- **71.4%** of employees reported increased productivity in open layouts (although only **44.2%** said the same locations).

B. **But Avoid the Pitfalls:** Eco, Distraction, Digital Distinction -Opening Office is not a silver tablet. The study shows:

- **70%** of offices have low divisions, but **50%** of workers say noise is their top distraction.
- Open layouts rather than avoiding noise violations, **70%** reduced the chat with people with emails.
- Stress, negative mood, errors, and even disease spikes in the open offices.
- Auditory dissatisfaction is real: noise disturbances and privacy loss predict emotional drain and disability.

C. **The Hybrid Sweet Spot: Enter the hybrid zone**: Open area for connection, private pods for concentrated work, and shared rooms for creativity. Just feel right? A recent journal of environmental psychology meta-analysis suggests that job satisfaction in a hybrid setup increases by **40%** and the turnover is reduced by **25%**.

A 2023 survey found that **77% of employees** want a mixed layout: open, private, and flexible zone. This is not just a preference-this is vital for productivity and welfare.

Crafting Collaborative Zones for Maximum Impact

Let us move from theory to design. How do you bring a supportive place into life?

1. **Welcome Areas & Breakout Nooks:**

   These act as creative Hothouses - Energy booster with no agenda.

   Examples:

   - **Soft seating** encourages comfort dialogue.
   - **Writable walls** invite thoughts at any time.
   - **Coffee stations** or green informal natural areas foster natural pauses.

Human senses matter. Pleasant meeting rooms (light, air quality, temperature) can increase productivity by **25%.** Do not ignore them.

2. **Meeting Rooms: Equipment for Creativity**

   Less rectangle, more arena:

   - **Circular tables** signal equality and easy thought flow.
   - **Adjustable Lighting** supports different modes -bright for thought-provocation, slow for idea reflection.
   - **Tech simplicity**: One-touch screen, wireless sharing, strong Wi-Fi. But make sure that there is no mess, no hindrance.

   Productivity decreases when meetings increase. But with the right environment, they shine.

3. **Private Pods for Deep Work**

   The focal zone needs focus. These pods:

   - They are soundproofed, visually cocooned.
   - Offer adjustables: chairs, desk heights, and lighting.
   - Integrate solutions: headphones, white noise, ergonomic design.

   They reduce around 21 minutes daily of distraction in open offices, and that is the reason why they're necessary.

4. **Transition Paths: Flow Is Experience**

   The spaces should guide the energy:

   - The **circulatory corridors** that move the atmosphere in a subtle way.
   - **Zoning**: Pitch → Associate Region → Focus Pods.
   - **Wayfinding design**: shift from floor wood to carpet; The walls are loudly transformed from art to a muted palette.

   The movement becomes part of the journey.

Case Studies That Feel Like Field Trips

1. **Steelcase Innovation Center:** This playground of solutions mixes treadmill pods, lounge chairs and privacy enclaves. They show that the cooperation of visitors does not require ping-pong,it requires thoughtful diversity.
2. **Cisco's Flexible Studio:**

   Cisco's hub labs are: retractable walls, AR tools, and adjustable zones. Their message? Cooperation is methodical and technology-enabled.
3. **Activity-Based Working (ABW): ABW** provides the activity zone per activity - focus, chat, and cooperate. This increases engagement and gives autonomy to employees. Both private and colleague zones are present.

Meeting Rooms and Breakout Spaces: UX > Aesthetics

- **Meetings That Matter:** Great meetings are built on great empathy, meaning spatial empathy too.
- **Booking ease:** Digital arrows, floor signage.
- **Room types:** From deep-think pods (dark, quiet, cushioned) to "loud labs" with whiteboards and energy.
- **Post-meeting care:** Storage, clean-up, recharge areas.
- **Breakout Areas That Inspire**

They should feel different, unexpected:

- **Visual contrast**: Playful murals, tangible textures.
- **Comfort first**: Lounge chairs, rugs, warm lighting.
- **Tech-light devices**: Tablets, post-its, sticky note boards.
- **The result**: relaxed minds unleash their best ideas.

Measuring Success: Numbers That Speak

How do you know it works?

1. **Usage data**: Are pods used? Who books what?
2. **Productivity metrics**: Focused work increases? Meetings shortened?
3. **Satisfaction surveys**: Are people energized, less stressed?
4. **Well-being indicators**: Illness down, engagement up?

Data-driven design = iterative design.

Common Hazards and How to Sidestep Them

- **Pitfall: All Open, All Problems:** Without privacy pods, open plans become noise prisons. Don't forget to build quiet zones.
- **Pitfall: Tech That Frustrates:** Love seeing people fumble with cables? No? Neither do visitors. Invest in flawless integration.
- **Pitfall: Zones Without Pressure:** Don't just create rooms: **Activate them**. Map their use, adjust lighting, make them versatile.

Final Word: Collaboration Works, If Designed Right

Collaboration is not an office blueprint - it is a combined environment of space, technology, and behavior. When thinking is ensured, the collaborative spaces become Idea engines, trust builders, and innovation centers.

Remember:

- Cooperation requires energy and retreat.
- Human senses matter - light, sound, texture, shape, experience.
- The use of spaces should not only be present: track, measurement, and adaptation.

Invest well in these areas, and you will see it - attached to action.

Chapter 6

Brand-Focused Design
Making Your Office an Extension of Your Identity

Your Space Should Speak Your Brand, Loud and Clear (But With Subtlety)

Your office is not where work is done - this is your brand, unplugged. It should include the values, culture, and story of your company without saying a word.

> **"A good design is a mix of aesthetics + basic human needs + wellbeing."**
>
> *– Ar. Pankaj Lad*

In this chapter, we are diving deeply into how we identify design channels, how to weave brand colors and materials, and how companies utilize their spaces as powerful marketing devices.

Design as a Mirror of Company Values and Culture

1. **From Mission Statement to Material Reality:** Imagine walking into a workplace where every surface and texture symbolizes "Innovation" or "Trust" - through subtle design signals. It is a brand-centric design. According to Frontier Interior Consultants, integrating persistent colors, furniture, and decorations that echo your values immediately aligns perception and behavior.

For example, an eco-conscious brand can lay down the usage of reclaimed wood, succulent greenery, and natural lighting, only to see "green", but to be green through experience. This stability reinforces culture - employees breathe it, customers rely on it.

2. **Embedding Culture in the Blueprint:** Visual brand cues are not limited to walls. Think of furniture layout, transparency, and circulation. Open areas speak transparency; Private glass offices suggest collaborative leadership; Natural lighting indicates openness and energy - all the main cultural DNAs.

   These spatial options strengthen the internal narrative. A tech-forward company may favor a flexible, multipurpose layout. A heritage-powered legal firm can rely on a mute tone and classic layout for calm professionalism.

Integrating Brand Colours, Materials & Storytelling

1. **Colours with Purpose:**

   Colour Psychology: Colour psychology is a potent tool. Blue builds trust; green evokes growth; yellow sparks energy. But the magic comes from strategic usage, accent walls in brand hues, branded graphics at eye level, and digital displays that cycle brand motifs. For instance, using a signature lilac accent (like Saie Beauty) in coworking zones bridges visual identity and emotional connection.

2. **Texture as Identity"**

   Think beyond colour: Textures activate the story. Velvet and wool signal warmth. Sleek wood surfaces convey authenticity. Glass and steel—modern transparency. Frontiers in office design highlight that layering textures gives depth and invites clients to feel your brand values.

3. **Storytelling Through Space**

   Every region should tell part of your story:

   - **Reception:** Brand Origin Illustration- Filled with its logo colors and motifs.
   - **Hallway:** Timeline canvas or provocative quotes describing milestones.
   - **Conference Room:** Branded Theme- "Innovation Room" specialty of patent milestone.
   - **Break area:** Interactive walls or company lore lounge where culture comes alive.

Software veteran Criteo embodies this beauty: global offices continuously share elements (a C-shaped barista counter, brand signage), but each regional office's materials, iconography, and even reflects local culture through vending displays.

4. **Environmental Graphics:** Data suggests that environmental graphics - local, typographic art, slogans - beautify; They behave majorly. Oh! The work of the studio designed for Dura

Roof shows corporate DNA -reinforcing values at every step with Etched "**Trust**" messages and integrated columns with room names.

Similarly, the studio AsA reminds us that the brand design should consider vision, sound, texture, even odour -even a holistic sensory experience is important.

> ***"Environment is one of the most important and influential factors of human evolution and continues to do so throughout its lifetime."***
>
> ***– Ar. Pankaj lad***

Crafting Your Office as a Marketing Tool

1. **The Silent Pitch:** Walk to the headquarters of Aesop and you will not see flashing advertisements. You will see a minimum, restrained location where thoughtfulness is the brand. This atmosphere generates discussion without saying a word - a form of silent marketing that is more effective than any billboard.
2. **Retail-Fusion Workspaces:** Aesop is an example - they have not only brought branding into offices, but they have also used retail elements in each field. Custom Finnish, Victorian details in Toronto, purpose-made furniture- places that are brand experiences.
3. **Digital Coating in Physical Form:** Digital-first brands are showing physical identity via thoughtful analog spaces. Studio O+A recommends analog creativity boosts—Facebook's analog lab and Yelp's war room counter pure digital to spark in-person engagement.

In a comparable way, Work & Co.'s offices in Portland and Copenhagen exemplify the brand's concept of minimalist efficiency by means of industrial structures, carefully selected accents, and flexible furniture.

Brands Living Their Identity

A Quick Dive Into Case Studies

1. **Criteo: Local Identity, Global Language:** Their branding changes in every global location. The Singapore office has online stall graphics; Tokyo Office, Neon Signage and Vending Machine; The Paris Office, Signature French Minimalism - all while a central brand axis (logo, reception counter) keeps it globally consistent.

3. **Aesop: Minimalism as Prestige:** A retailer that never advertised, they became distinguished through understanding in every new store or scripture through a compatible design. Their headquarters and shops showcase the honor of the Victorian era, ceramics, brass, and muted tones, all of which are drawn from locals and brands.

4. **Saie Beauty: Sustainable Identity:** Their Tribeca head quarters mixed the Scandinavian style with neutral tones with neutral tones with natural, durable elements such as vintage wood, brand lilac accents-systematically shifting between all the workspaces and retail showrooms.

5. **Frog: Heritage Reimagined:** The headquarters of the frog reflects its own design mission - an Apple Mac SE is displayed in an art installation, a handcrafted kitchen, and Bespoke brand elements that remind visitors of their heritage of design innovation.

Sensory Branding: Engage Beyond Sight

Visual branding only scratches the surface. Five senses provide a rich story.

- **Fragrance** memory and emotion. Think about the imperative of conscience associated with the identity of Custom Aroma or the Brand of Singapore Airlines.
- The ambient playlist's brand-relevant **sound** supports the brand's approach.
- **Touch and texture** produce emotional engagement - Hardwood, linen surfaces, and sculpture elements make depth.

In conclusion, sensory branding drives loyalty, memory, and builds deep connections.

Creating Visual Brand Language in Space

Visual Brand Language 101

This factor is about colour, finish, and character, which directly affects the subconscious mind. BMW's Grill, Starbucks' icon, Curated Room Theme of Airbnb- Breathing Views create immediate recognition.

In office design, bring your brand toolkit to life: Graphics, typography, custom iconography, UI-style signing that speaks about your brand's UX, and geometry.

From Toolkit to Execution

- Define core items like color palette, finish, material texture, typography, and icon set.
- Roll them into zone-specific use-like, near the statement wall + audio activation reception.
- Ensure that every detail matches the identity - from the mug to the pad.

Your Office Is the Ultimate Brand Touchpoint

Think of your office as the most frequent brand canvas. It welcomes, indicates, reinforces, and sells - all without speaking. It is a symbol of values and identity. If you design with intentions, your office becomes a silent ambassador - client converting, energetic teams, and telling your story - 24/7.

⦸⦸⦸⦸

Chapter 7

The Business of Productivity

Optimizing Your Workspace for Success

Productivity Isn't an Accident; It's Engineered.

In the results business, efficiency is the final ROI benchmark. But the output does not appear only with open laptops and caffeine - it is engineered through the very design of your workspace. Every air vent, desktop space, and curve in the corridor matters. In this chapter, we unpack:

1. **How layout shapes efficiency and workflow**
2. **Ergonomics- silent productivity multiplier**
3. **Science of light, sounds, and air quality**

Let's turn your office into a productivity powerhouse - a design option at a time.

Layout & Efficiency: The Invisible Flow

1. **Task-Based Zoning:** A workpiece should respect how people actually work. Studies suggest that facilities by placing features - the flow within the desk of secular, coffee, collaborative zones can cut disruptions up to **15%**. Workflow becomes comfortable, not interrupted.
2. **Smart Seat Pairing:** It turns out, your office neighbour matters. Harvard researchers found that groups of

"**Producers**" and "**Quality**" employees increase overall productivity between **13%** to **17%**.

3. **The Dos and Don'ts of Hot-Desking:** Hot-desking promises flexibility, but often brings stress and confusion. Wired reported that it wastes time to find seats and creates friction between teams. If you become flexible, add wayfinding, locker, and seat-regulation tools to reduce chaos.

Ergonomics: The Untapped Asset

1. **Chairs That Work With You:** Relaxation is an efficiency booster, not a luxury. A global survey found that **34%** of employees cite back pain from chairs as a major issue. Ergonomic chairs reduce fatigue and promote productivity, not to forget the mention of the reduction in absence.
2. **Adjustable Workspaces:** Modern work demands adaptability. Sit -Stand Desk, Footrest, and Monitor Arms empower users to transfer posture throughout the day. This diversity is not trivial-it maintains the brain and body sharp and combats monotonous errors.

3. **Reduce Micro-Discomfort:** Even small pain disrupts the flow. A study by the University of Calgary shows that noise, stress, and even poorly lit corners lead to lost productivity and sick days. Ergonomics intentionally combats this subtle disintegration with design.

A short story: When Rehan Mehta reached out, his IT startup was growing fast, but so was absenteeism due to back and neck issues. I did a quick assessment and immediately spotted the problem: poor ergonomics. We replaced their rigid setups with adjustable chairs, sit-stand desks, and wider workstations. Sick leaves dropped by **50%** within three months, and their sprint velocity jumped. Rehan told me, "I used to think this stuff was fancy. Turns out, it's foundational."

Lighting: More Than a Lamp

1. **Natural Light = Brain Power:** Sunlight is not just a decorative factor - its performance is like energy. A journal of environmental psychology cites a **20%** uplift in productivity after redesigning the spaces for daylight. Several studies show that exposure to sufficient natural light decreases tiredness by 56%, migraines by 63%, and eye strain by 51%.

   But recently, technological developments have led to the invention of "**Human Centric Lights**" that mimic natural light, which act and help just like natural light and have similar effects on human psychology and productivity.

   We experimented with lights at Sparklinx Solutions, which is a tech startup, where we replaced the LED lights with HCL (Human Centric Lights), and the company saw a jump in productivity within the first week, and even employees accepted that their overall work focus increased by **25%**.

2. **Combat Glare and Flicker:** Bright light is good, but the harsh glare isn't. According to light ergonomics standards, illumination levels, proper contrast, absence of flicker, and balanced temperature prevent errors, eye strain, and bad moods.

   Light has a significant effect on employees' brains; compared to artificial lighting, exposure to natural light can increase decision-making by **42%**, improve sleep by **37 minutes**, and increase productivity by up to **18%**. Lack of daylight, on the other hand, is associated with poorer sleep, less physical activity, and a decline in mood and cognitive function. While too much blue light at night can delay melatonin release by up to **1.5 hours**, which disrupts sleep and morning alertness, blue-enriched illumination during shifts improves alertness and decreases reaction times.

Acoustics: The Overlooked Efficiency Factor

1. **Open Offices Aren't Always Pleasant:** The New Yorker reported that open offices lower attention spans, raise stress hormones, and increase sickness leaves by over **60%**. Productivity is thus lost as soon as privacy disappears.
2. **The Cost of Distraction:** Multitalker distraction in open offices lowers cognitive performance-sometimes to the extent of **15%**-and subjective distraction rises sharply as noise builds.
3. **Quiet Computing Saves the Day:** Here comes the tranquil zones, acoustic panels, private pods, and white noise masking. This fortunate knowledge comes from a **2020 Steelcase global survey**, which showed that **85%** of employees valued concentration without interruptions; a direct solution of creating quiet zones answers both retention and satisfaction.
4. **Material Choices Matter:** In the acoustics world, existing materials matter: carpet and ceiling absorption accomplish a 2–4 dB level quieter atmosphere than those without. Offices that carry this acoustic treatment are measured to have increased focus and calm.

Model Case Study: Regina Thomas had built a beautiful wellness startup—but her open-plan office was killing focus. I diagnosed the acoustic problem immediately. We brought in sound-absorbing panels, lush indoor plants, and carved out quiet zones. The impact was clear: productivity rose by **25%**, and team stress dropped significantly. Regina told me, "The silence you created is full of clarity."

Air Quality & Thermal Comfort: Hidden ROI

1. **Ventilation Drives Health:** WELL and ASHRAE standards say that better ventilation, e.g., increased fresh-air flow rates,

will increase cognitive performance by about **10%** while reducing building-related illness by nearly **19%**.

2. **Temperature = Attention:** Performance is influenced by thermal comfort; individuals get distracted by fluctuations in climate. Zoned HVAC control and fan-assisted cooling may minimize discomfort resulting from temperature variations in different regions.
3. **Breathe Well, Work Better:** Headaches, fatigue, and vision problems are all related to bad indoor air quality. Bring in low-VOC materials, monitor air quality actively, add plants, and follow clean-air protocols for positive results.

Model Case Study: Jignesh Patel's team was burning out—frequent coughs, fatigue, and low morale. I visited their warehouse and found stagnant air, dust build-up, and poor ventilation. We added HEPA filters, created airflow corridors, and built better ventilation zones. Within weeks, sick days dropped by **40%**. Jignesh called it a turning point: "The air changed, and so did the energy of our team."

Biophilia & Wellbeing Zones: Recharging Brainpower

1. **Green in, Stress Out:** Bring in a few plants to make the space lively. What would have otherwise been a boring office space without it, and you will get a **15%** productivity increase. The biophilic design, with plants, natural sunlight, and textures, tends to repair the mind and foster performance.
2. **Dedicated Recharge Spaces:** Having quiet rooms, mini gyms, and nap pods, the list goes on, are not perks. Instead, these are tools for productivity. According to research on office framework, wellness zones can reduce stress-related problems by **30%** and boost efficiency by an additional **20%**.

Performance Approach: Evaluate, Improve, Recur

1. **Track What Matters:** Leverage booking data, productivity outcome, medical records, or health log, and satisfaction surveys to measure the space performance. Almost **83%** of organized workers wake up every day claiming that their setup improves their productivity by **38%**.

2. **Pilot & Iterate:**

   Go small: Deploy one or two quiet pods and some ergonomic chairs, then survey and adjust accordingly. These little mini-experiments will ensure you keep scaling your improvements without heavy upfront investments.

3. **Listen to the Body:**

   Frequently check: Are headaches down? Are errors fewer? Are sick days lower? These human metrics reveal true ROI.

Productivity by Design

Each element matters when assessing office design as a performance lever. Being productive requires more than just functioning; it additionally includes integrating comfort, flow, and clarity into daily tasks.

It is paradoxical to have an efficient office that seems productive. Using this layered approach backed by science can create harmony between workflow, wellness, and the results.

⦸⦸⦸⦸

Chapter 8

Office Design Mistakes That Cost Businesses Millions

The High-Stakes Price of Getting It Wrong

Office design is no more a question of aesthetics but rather of business: an office design may build or break productivity and morale, and thereby the value of the business. Making a mess of the office entails huge costs: lost productivity, disengaged employees, lost opportunities, and costly renovations.

The Most Expensive Mistakes

1. **Designing Without Input from Real Users:** Designing an office without involving employees is almost like baking a cake without knowing the ingredients. Even if it seems good, it won't function. Employees are the primary users of a space, and overlooking their needs leads to dissatisfaction, poor performance, and even ROI turnover.

   Smart Move: Get the staff involved early on. Surveys, interviews, and pilot zones give real-world insight into what works and what does not.

2. **Poor Space Planning:** When offices are too cramped or too roomy, they generate costs and loss of productivity. Very tight spaces tend to increase stress and deny collaboration. In very spacious offices, however, the budget sinks with operational costs, but they contribute little.

Smart Move: Employ the professional planners and space utilization software to test all traffic flow and adjust the space to your own team dynamics.

3. **Prioritizing Style Over Function:** A slick modern office with nothing going for work is just style. Popular designs often skimp on important functional components such as noise control, private spaces, and usable technology.

   Model Case Study: Neha Arora was struggling to keep her warehouse team aligned. Orders were getting delayed, returns were messy, and the place felt chaotic. I reimagined the entire space using lean principles—clear zoning for packing, returns, and dispatch. We widened aisles, reduced clutter, and simplified navigation. The result? Order processing time was halved, and customer satisfaction soared. Neha told me, "It finally feels like a system, not a scramble."

   Smart Move: Let the functionality dictate. Venture into focus pods, hubs of collaboration, and furniture designed around actual tasks.

4. **Ignoring Lighting, Acoustics, and Air Quality:** Lighting, acoustics, and air quality are the backbone of performance: poor lighting causes fatigue, poor air increases sick days, and excess noise reduces focus and morale.

   Smart Move: Allow natural light, but balance it with task lighting. Invest in noise masking and acoustic panels. Look for LEED or WELL HVAC standards.

5. **No Room for Growth or Change:** An unjustifiably rigid design will age fast. As your company grows and changes, so should the spaces available to it. More expensive are permanent constructs and static layouts that cannot be changed later.

   Smart Move: Go with a modular design. Movable walls, multi-use spaces, and scalable tech will greatly reduce your renovation needs down the road.

Form Without Function: The Hidden Danger

1. **Trying Too Hard:** Design for a "**WOW**" without any substance: the office has too many features, colors, or gimmicks as poor distractions for an employee.

   Smart Move: Keep it simple-inviting. Mix statement pieces with neutral tones and predefined zones.

2. **Fast Fading Fads:** Trendy ones like open layout and full-on hot-desking are destined to flop if implemented without considering satisfaction. They appear innovative but grieve workers without context.

   Smart Move: See what works with your team's work habits. Test-drive some concepts before full-scale implementation.

3. **Confusing Spaces Kill Collaboration:** Confusion reigns with a lack of zoning. Employees do not know where to concentrate or where to disgorge their thoughts, or just unwind. Ambiguities take time.

Smart Move: Visual differentiation of zones by way of floor, lighting, and furniture from one another. Clear labeling of spaces. In fact, they must provide a mix of areas for focus as well as social interactions.

Future-Proofing 101

1. **Flexibility as Foundation:** Your workforce and needs will be altered. A future-ready office can be modified easily without costly construction.

   Wise Move: Purchase furnishings that are click-together, flexible partitions, and open utility access points.

2. **Tech Integration:** With the help of real-time information from IoT sensors, intelligent lighting, and workspace analytics tools, you can make design changes, environmental adjustments, and energy-waste optimizations.

   Wise Move: Begin with a single smart zone and multiply from there. Prefer systems that offer mobile accessibility along with information dashboards.

3. **Sustainability = Smarter Investment:** Expressing commitment to sustainability through the office environment is just one side of it. On the other hand, it provides possibilities for savings over the long term. Biophilic design, reused items, and sustainable HVAC enhance the potential for return on the money you put in.

   Wise Move: Set up some recycling areas, add some greenery, and select certified products.

4. **Hybrid Work Compatibility:** Both remote and in-person teammates must be assisted by the office. The new normal is hybrid, as it has become much more than just a trend.

   Wise Move: Ready-to-use video-capable rooms for meetings, hot desks that may be reserved, and seamless internet access in any area.

5. **Inclusion and Wellness Built-In:** In settings designed for everybody, different groups flourish. Ergonomic places of work, bathrooms that are gender-neutral, and wellness areas truly reflect that you care.

   Model Case Study: Harpreet Singh noticed his café staff dragging their feet—burnout was setting in. I designed wellness corners with yoga mats, hydration hubs, and pockets of natural light. Monday morning attendance improved, and energy levels soared throughout the week. Harpreet smiled and said, "When our people feel good, the food tastes better too."

Smart Move: Install accessible paths, quiet areas, and flexible desks. Prioritize wellness when designing your creative approach.

From Cost Center to Profit Engine

Predictable Returns

- Better lighting, arrangements, and dynamics lead to improved productivity.
- Lower turnover due to wellness-forward design
- Improved brand equity with advanced technology and environmentally friendly aspects

Real Value: Companies with well-designed workplaces claim a **25%** higher rate in employee performance and a **30%** higher rate for client perceptions of professionalism.

Real-World Successes

- **WeWork:** Provides space for movable lounges and differing layouts to encourage engagement
- **Spotify:** Has areas supporting mental health, creativity, and privacy.
- **JLL:** Built flexible, sustainable, and data-driven spaces as they evolve together with their clients

Your Smart Design Checklist:

Avoid These Pitfalls

1. No user research done
2. Overcrowded or empty zones
3. Looks great, works terribly
4. Poor air, light, or sound quality
5. Fixed features, no flexibility

6. No green or inclusive design elements
7. Not ready for hybrid work

If you checked more than two from the above list, you're leaking money.

The Bottom Line

Office interior design is a business strategy; treat it as such. Prevent pitfalls by designing with purpose and not ego. Flexibility, wellness, and user experience certainly ought to be your guiding lights. In doing so, you will not only be saving money, but you will be developing a future-proof, high-functioning company that draws in top talent and keeps them motivated.

⃠⃠⃠⃠

Chapter 9

Stakeholder Experience - Designing for Those Who Matter Most: Clients, Employees & Investors

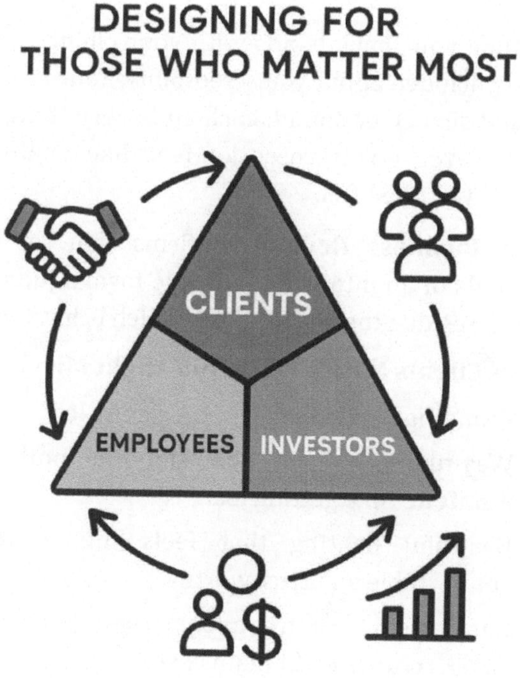

A workplace is not merely an office; it is a signal.

It tells clients what their partner in business is. It tells the employees how much a company values their welfare. To investors, it says more about agility, thoughtfulness, and being future-ready. So why should anyone design for the walls and windows only, when the design could be for **human experience**?

Let us analyze how the space becomes a stage theatre for three key stakeholders in brand survival: Client, Employee, and Investor.

Part I: The Client Experience: Trust at First Glance

Perception Is Positioning

By the time you shake hands with your client, they might have already concluded about your credibility. Your lobby, your mix of scents and silence or sound, each and every thing shouts, "**This is who we are.**" If your reception feels like an afterthought to a budget, so will the offer.

Harvard Business Review confirms that, in the first few milliseconds of an interaction, people form a judgment, and the emotional residue thereof is sticky, which is hard to reverse later.

- **What Clients Notice (That You Might Miss):**
  - Branding beyond logos; experience-led
  - Way-finding should be smooth; nothing says "**An amateur**" like getting lost
  - Beautiful lighting that feels immersive, while still comfortable and trustworthy.
  - Furniture or wall treatment, whether custom-made, that speaks craft, or just plain cost.

- **Tactics to Instantly Impress:**
  - Design a "**welcome corridor**" wherein pace slows down and soothes
  - Use materials that shout out your value (brushed brass, real wood, MDF). Client-side tech, such as touchscreen directories and digital walls of art, should be incorporated. One hospitality gesture would do: scent, barista-grade espresso, a curated playlist.

Clients don't want to feel like visitors. They want to feel **expected**.

Part II: The Employee Experience — Culture Made Tangible

Why Space = Engagement

Employees don't care about yet another 'cool' office... with a ping-pong table that no one ever uses. What your team wants is purpose. Autonomy. Respect. Smart office design is such a silent handshake between you and your employees, whispering: "**We've thought about you.**"

The **2023 Gensler Workplace Survey** reveals its well-designed office employees to be 2x more innovative and **31%** more productive.

- **What Modern Teams Actually Value:**
    - Natural light & greenery (biophilic design is no buzzword, it is biology)
    - Space variety: quiet booths, creative huddle spots, recharge zones.
    - Air quality, temperature control, and low-noise zones.
    - Subtle branding: spaces that inspire pride, not pressure.
- **Culture-First Design Tactics:**
    - **Create culture alleys**: Halls or walls that showcase the team's wins and stories.
    - **Color psychology**: Use color psychology with green being calm, blue focusing, and yellow energizing.
    - **Provide adjustable seating**: The place of choice shows diversity and trust.

- **Layer in texture**: Acoustic panels, relaxing furniture, and an inviting design.

Designed for people, not job titles. Every nook should have a reason, and someone it exists for.

Part III: The Investor Experience: Proof in Physical Form

From Pitch to Portfolio

Investors are not seeing spreadsheets anymore; they see how your space performs. Is it built for Scale? Is it efficient? Is it well aligned with the Brand? Your office is a risk signal or a value driver.

A **Deloitte 2022 Real Estate Trends** report found that investors in the post-COVID situation look at "adaptive space use" and "brand alignment" when deciding to invest.

- **What Investors Look For:**
- Mindful use of real estate (no ghost spaces or intentional cost emptiness)
- Illustration of physical as well as digital connectivity with dashboards in real time,
- Does your space communicate the same idea as your pitch deck with respect to design?
- Advocates sustainable practices and credentials (LEED, WELL, Fitwel)
- **How to Design Keeping ROI in Mind:**
    - "Show multi-use ROI spaces": meeting room in the morning, lounge in the night.
    - Feature performance data: screen displays of energy usage, space statistics

- The office aligns with future-of-work trends: modular design, hybrid tool set-up
- Include a "**Vision Gallery**": a space that visually ideates your strategy.

Investors finance companies that are future-proof and design tells them if you are ready.

Part IV: The Sweet Spot: Where All Three Overlap

The Power of Shared Experience

Trust, talent, and traction: A service design that harnesses these values for clients, employees, and investors.

- The glass-walled team room? Showcases your collaborative culture
- The eco-certified HVAC system? Comfort for employees + ESG gold for investors.
- The interactive welcome wall? That wows clients and says "you're important" to employees.
- **Three Universal Design Truths:**

1. **Transparency builds trust** - across all stakeholders
2. **Flexibility builds confidence** - showing adaptation capabilities.
3. **Details are declarations** - the small stuff matters to clients, teams, and investors.

Experience by Design: Your Stakeholder Checklist

Before you lay tile or paint a wall, run your concept through this stakeholder experience filter:

Element	Clients	Employees	Investors
Arrival Experience	Clear signage, welcome tech	Comfy entry with seating	Security + tech transparency
Work Zones	Impressive but not excessive	Task-specific + hybrid-friendly	Efficient use of space
Meeting Spaces	Professional, tech-forward	Private + collaborative options	Scalable, smart-integrated
Brand Storytelling	Visual & tactile brand identity	Inspirational internal messaging	Consistency with mission/ vision
Amenities	Hospitality-level touchpoints	Wellness zones, recharge areas	Sustainable, practical additions

Designing with Depth

Forget surface design. Today's best offices don't impress with size or shine—they win with **meaningful experience**.

Design every space as if your top client is about to visit, your best team member is deciding whether to stay, and your next investor is touring for the first time.

Chapter 10

The Future of Office Design: Where Trends Are Heading

The office, once the symbol of corporate control, is now a canvas of evolution. It's no longer just where people work; it's how they work, what keeps them coming back, and why they show up. As technology, climate, and culture reshape our world, so too must our offices change from static spaces into adaptive environments.

Let's leap forward. The future of work demands more than Wi-Fi and beanbags; therefore, this chapter addresses the new design ideas, trends, and innovations that will guide the next generation of work environments.

Hybrid Is Here to Stay, But Not As You Think

The New Normal: Choice-Driven Design

The hybrid work environment is a competitive benefit rather than an arrangement that compromises. After the pandemic, workers desire independence, alternatives, and a sense of purpose. This involves developing environments that promote attendance as opposed to compelling it.

McKinsey (2023) indicates that although **87%** of workers favor working hours that are flexible, just **31%** think their current workplace fosters them.

Design Implications:

- Neighborhood layouts instead of fixed desks
- Purpose-built collaboration zones, not makeshift meeting corners
- Remote-optimized rooms with smart lighting, mics, and cameras
- Desk hoteling systems for seamless seat booking

Becoming adaptable is the foundation of relevance, not just a fashion statement.

Tech-Infused Workspaces: Smarter Than Ever

AI + IoT = Intelligent Offices

Envision your office altering its temperature, illumination, and even the resonance depending on the time of day and the individuals using that area. We're not far away from such times.

Deployment of smart offices improves productivity by **16%** and decreases maintenance costs by up to **30%**, based on another **Deloitte (2022)** study.

- **What's Trending:**
- IoT sensors for occupancy, temperature, and air quality
- Digital twins—virtual models of physical spaces for live data monitoring
- AI-powered facility management for energy savings and predictive maintenance
- AR/VR meeting rooms for immersive remote collaboration

The future isn't just automated. It's anticipatory.

Wellness is the New Productivity

Biophilic & Holistic Design Goes Mainstream

Offices that nourish the human body and soul will outperform. Advantages are no longer significant; instead, the focus is on encouraging identity, enhancing cognitive health, and avoiding burnout.

Based on data collected by the WELL Building Institute, companies that emphasize well-being in their design embrace **12%** fewer sick days and **28%** higher employee retention statistics.

Vital Trends in Wellness:

- Circadian lighting systems that synchronize with the phases created by nature
- Indoor greenery + natural materials for cognitive restoration
- On-site recharge rooms and mental health pods
- Antibacterial and intangible materials for a clean layout

Design is far more than visual appeal. It all comes down to what is ethically, mentally, and naturally right.

Sustainability Is Normalized

From LEED Badges to Built-In Purpose

Sustainability is no longer optional. It's expected by employees, demanded by clients, and scrutinized by investors. Offices must now embody ESG goals, not just echo them.

The **World Green Building Council** estimates that green buildings conserve energy consumption by **50%**, water usage by **25%**, and greenhouse gases by **34%**.

Sustainable Design Innovations:

- Modular walls and decor to increase mobility and cut unnecessary waste
- Renewable and thermal energy-powered zero-carbon structures
- Harvesting of rainwater and smart HVAC systems
- Materials transparency, knowing where every product comes from

Green isn't a paint color—it's a design language for the 21st century.

Neurodiversity & Comprehensiveness Take Center Stage

Design for All Minds and Bodies

Diversification, both mental and physical, will be valued in the future business. This includes areas that are appropriate for wheelchair users, individuals with sensory issues, Morning people and night owls, and introverts and extroverts.

As stated by the British Council for Offices (2022), teamwork and efficiency have a direct link with design that is inclusive.

Inclusive Design Moves:

- Quiet zones and sensory rooms for neurodivergent employees
- Height-adjustable counters, automatic doors, tactile signage
- Visual and acoustic zoning for choice-based engagement
- Universal restrooms and spiritual spaces

True innovation is inclusive by default, not retrofitted after the fact.

Hospitality Meets Work: "Resimercial" 2.0

The era of could be smoother as **"resimercial, which combines commercial operations with residential comfort"**, is here. Offices now offer café aesthetics, concierge services, and lounge-style meeting rooms.

A recent CBRE report shows that hospitality-style offices lead to **23%** higher employee satisfaction and stronger client engagement.

What That Looks Like:

- Crafted coffee houses, cozy couches, and well-chosen music
- Fragrance designed to elevate mood and memory
- Curated art & storytelling installations that reflect company culture
- Amenity-rich spaces: showers, nap pods, meditation rooms

The goal? Instead of making the office a duty, make it a destination.

The Algorithm-Driven Office: Data-Backed Everything

Analytics + Empathy = Optimal Spaces

Design's future is backed by real-time data rather than just following trends. Analytics are utilized in smart offices to learn how people use the environment, where resources go to waste, and how to improve faster.

As reported by Verdantix (2023), companies that used workplace analytics applications saw a **32%** increase in space utilization and a **20%** reduction in expenses.

Data in Design:

- Heat maps to track foot traffic
- Behavioral analytics to adjust layouts
- Space sentiment surveys fed into AI dashboards
- Digital feedback tools for continual design iteration

In short: the office of tomorrow isn't just observed—it's learning.

The Metaverse & Virtual Office Overlay

Offices Without Borders

While physical offices evolve, the digital workplace explodes. Virtual reality, holograms, and metaverse integrations allow workers to collaborate, ideate, and build community, even across continents.

Meta and Accenture partnered in 2022 to build metaverse-based onboarding programs, reducing traditional onboarding costs by **30%** and time required for the same process by **40%**.

Hybrid Virtual-Physical Blends:

- AR overlays for presentations that are interactive in real-world spaces
- Digital twin offices accessible from anywhere
- Virtual water coolers and avatar-led meetings
- Blockchain-secured access and document storage

This isn't just science fiction. It's a new dimension of workplace culture.

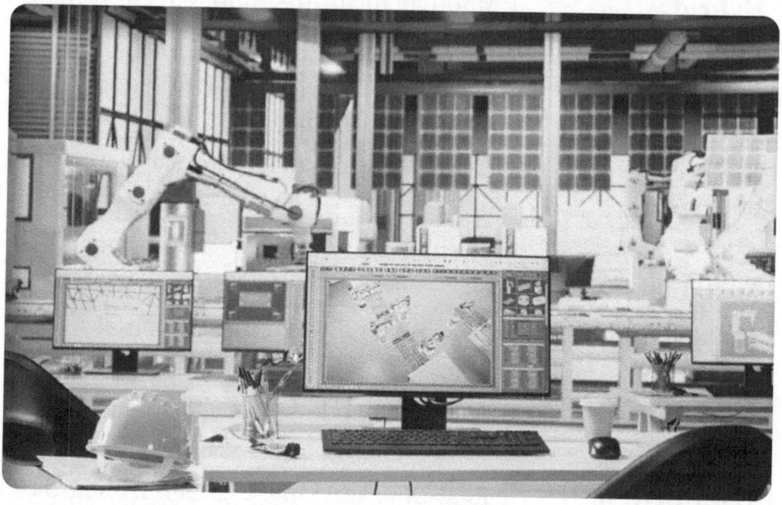

Future Design's Timeless Constants

Certain rules remain consistent amidst changing trends:

1. People should be regarded when building technologies, not as a way of eliminating them.
2. Storytelling wins; your office must express your *why*

3. Agility beats grandeur, spaces must evolve, not just impress
4. Function + Emotion, successful spaces make people *feel* something

The future office is not a finish line; it's an interface between culture, commerce, and consciousness.

Your 2030 Office Design Playbook

Design Principle	Future Action
Hybrid Enablement	Modular furniture, mobile tech, zoning strategies
Smart Integration	AI HVAC, occupancy sensors, predictive lighting
Wellness Centricity	Biophilia, acoustic comfort, ergonomic diversity
ESG & Sustainability	Circular materials, net-zero targets, energy AI
Inclusive by Design	Neuro-friendly layouts, universal access
Hospitality Touchpoints	Concierge-style service, ambient environments
Data-Driven Flexibility	Real-time tracking, digital dashboards
Virtual Layer Integration	AR/VR tools, digital twins, virtual onboarding

How to Get Office Design Right

The basis of an excellent office is purpose, flow, and functioning, not sleek furniture or up-to-date schemes of color. The finest work stations improve efficiency, communicate your brand's traits, and help every client remember your principles and identity. By eliminating common errors and embracing the tactics outlined in this book, you're not only establishing an office; you're shaping the trajectory of the business you run.

This is the time to turn your workspace's four walls into your boldest business statement ever. Are you ready to design your edge?

Now the question is: **Why have me by your side/trust me**?

The answer is: Because I went through all this the **hard way**.

Because I have made **mistakes**, and from them, built systems to ensure they will never happen again.

Because I have sat on every side of a project: **design, client, contractor, and mentor**.

Because this book did not come from high above a pedestal: it came from the trenches. From an architect who has been in the field for more than two and a half decades and is still working successfully and his experience involved with contracts and founder, where he saw a pattern emerging: most office spaces look decent on drawings but fail to really perform.

Because I still wake up every single day, pencil in hand, chasing that very question I asked in school:

"How can we make this space work better?"

- If you have ever felt adrift in your **office project**, consider this book your compass.
- If you have ever been **burned by a designer**, consider this book your **second chance**.
- If you believe your workplace can do **better**, consider this book your **blueprint**.
- Let's redesign not just your office—but how you think about design.
- Let's build with **clarity, conviction, and creativity**.

Let me tell you about Mr. Gupta, an experienced businessman who came to me facing the same hardship. His office was working, but barely. Visitors felt all boxed up, employees were feeling demotivated, and cash flow was quietly bleeding away.

Now, here is what we did for him, and here is what you will come to learn in this book:

- **Slashed capex** through *value-engineering* methods that retained visual appeal but cut out financial waste
- **Reduced operational costs** by planning air flow, lighting, and layout the right way, not the expensive way
- **Boosted staff morale** by designing a **café-inspired entrance** that banished **Monday blues** at the door
- **Created multifunctional zones,** a single space that could transform from meeting room to ideation hub to casual breakout area
- **Used minimal furniture, placed smartly,** with curved forms that added both flow and spatial depth

- **Selected value-for-money materials** that looked high-end because they were placed *where they mattered most*
- **Increased openness** with double-height ceilings, avoiding the typical claustrophobic office trap
- **Amplified brand identity,** not with logo wallpaper, but with experiences, textures, and finishes that *spoke to the brand*
- And most importantly, we made his office **work *harder than ever before,*** without spending harder

This book will walk you through these strategies and more, not in theory, but through **actionable methods, proven frameworks, and mistakes to avoid**.

So, if you're:

- Spending **more** but getting **less**
- Unsure how to reflect your **brand** in your space
- Losing **talent** to better-designed competitors
- Drowning in **WhatsApp suggestions** from acquaintances-turned-interior-experts
- Or simply stuck staring at your current office, wondering why it doesn't feel "**right**".

Then this book is your breakthrough.

Exercise - **"Visualize the energy, design the space, manifest a workspace where your goals come to life."**

You didn't pick up *The Office Design Trap* just to read.

- You picked it up to **rise.**
- To elevate your business.
- To shape a legacy and your vision.
- To design a workspace that inspires innovation, wellness, and unstoppable momentum.

Now, you've got two choices:

1. **Keep your space stuck in survival mode.**
2. **Or design for 10X growth, clarity, and real impact.**

Let's unlock your next big win together.

Book your free virtual strategy session now.

Your breakthrough office, your boldest vision, it starts here.

[Connect with us on admin@sarayan.com for a session]

⦸⦸⦸⦸

References

1. **Gensler (2023)**: *U.S. Workplace Survey:* Details the impact of office design on productivity, collaboration, and brand identity.

   [Source: www.gensler.com]

2. **Harvard Business Review (2019)**: *The Impact of Physical Space on Business Outcomes*

   Covers environmental psychology, first impressions, and design's influence on trust and decision-making.

   [Source: hbr.org]

3. **Steelcase (2022)**: *The Science of Workplace Design*

   Research-based insights on how lighting, ergonomics, and layout affect employee morale and efficiency.

   [Source: www.steelcase.com]

4. **Susan M. Winchip (2011)**: *Interior Design: A Critical Introduction*

   Explores the difference between aesthetics and function in interior design with real-world application.

   [ISBN: 978-1609010690]

5. **IDEO & Tim Brown (2009)**: *Change by Design*

   Discusses design thinking, the value of human-centered space planning, and its business relevance.

   [ISBN: 978-0061766084]

6. **MSME Day 2025:** Empowering India's Economic Backbone

   [Source:https://www.pib.gov.in/PressNoteDetails.aspx?id=154772&NoteId=154772&ModuleId=3]

7. **Apple Park Design Case Study (ArchDaily, 2017)**
Highlights Apple's use of minimalism and brand philosophy in architectural expression. [Source: www.archdaily.com]

8. **Goldman Sachs HQ Profile (Dezeen, 2018)**
Covers the blend of legacy and modernity in Goldman Sachs' office interiors. [Source: www.dezeen.com]

9. **Googleplex Design Analysis (Fast Company, 2020)**
Details Google's unconventional design choices and their impact on innovation culture.
[Source: www.fastcompany.com]

10. **Amazon Office Culture Study (Business Insider, 2017)**
Explains Amazon's utilitarian and cost-effective design approach and its cultural messaging.
[Source: www.businessinsider.com]

11. **Environmental Psychology of Design (Mehrabian & Russell, 1974)** – *An Approach to Environmental Psychology*
Fundamental psychological theories about how spatial environments influence human behavior.
[ISBN: 978-0262630433]

12. **Gensler (2023)**: *Global Workplace Survey*
Covers how workplace design influences emotions, engagement, and memorability. [Source: www.gensler.com]

13. **Steelcase (2023)**: *Global Workplace Report*
Reports that design directly impacts satisfaction, creativity, and productivity. [Source: www.steelcase.com]

14. **Gallo, Carmine (2014)**: *Talk Like TED*
Explains how novelty activates the brain's reward system and improves retention.
[ISBN: 978-1250041128]

15. **Journal of Interior Design, Vol. 45 (2021)**: *Experiential Design in the Workplace*

Defines experiential design and its role in emotional branding through space. [Source: Wiley Online Library]

16. **Dezeen (2022)**: *Airbnb Office Design Tour*

Case study on Airbnb HQ, where rooms are modeled on actual listings to amplify the brand story.

[Source: www.dezeen.com]

17. **Work Design Magazine (2021)**: *Spotify NYC Office Tour*

Describes how curated audio at entry reinforces brand and creates a multisensory first impression.

[Source: www.workdesign.com]

18. **Office Snapshots (2019)**: *Dropbox HQ Design*

Case study showing how layout flow enhances employee experience and cognitive refreshment.

[Source: www.officesnapshots.com]

19. **Spangenberg et al. (2016)**: *Journal of Environmental Psychology*

Research on how scent significantly influences spatial perception and emotional response.

[DOI: 10.1016/j.jenvp.2016.01.005]

20. **Wired (2017)**: *Inside Twitter HQ*

Review of intentional design elements like tweet murals that fuse branding and architecture.

[Source: www.wired.com]

21. **Architectural Digest (2023)**: *Salesforce Tower Art and Brand Identity*

Documents Salesforce's use of intentional art curation to communicate brand values.

[Source: www.architecturaldigest.com]

22. **University of California, Irvine (2018)**: *Acoustics and Focus Study*

Shows how predictable soundscapes reduce distraction and boost concentration. [Source: www.uci.edu]

23. **IDEO (2021)**: *Design Thinking Toolkit*

Offers strategies for emotional design through user-centric environments. [Source: www.ideo.com]

24. **Chapman, Jonathan (2005)**: *Emotionally Durable Design*

Discusses design longevity and the emotional value of restraint in luxury. [ISBN: 978-1844071811]

25. **Wired (2017)**: *Apple Park Review*

Exploration of Apple Park's seamless, minimalist design and architectural philosophy. [Source: www.wired.com]

26. **Sleep Review Magazine**: "Circadian Science: Why Natural Light Makes for Better Workers"

https://sleepreviewmag.com/sleep-health/circadian-science-natural-light-better-workers/

27. **National Institutes of Health (NIH)**: "Impact of Windows and Daylight Exposure on Overall Health and Sleep Quality"

https://www.ncbi.nlm.nih.gov/pmc/articles/PMC4031400/

28. **London School of Economics (2018)**: *Behavioral Research Lab Study*

Examines how luxury cues in space influence perception of trust and brand prestige. [Source: www.lse.ac.uk]

29. **Barrett, P., Zhang, Y., Davies, F., & Barrett, L. (2013)**: *Building and Environment*

Finds that spatial impressions are formed within 1/10th of a second, impacting perception. [DOI: 10.1016/j.buildenv.2012.09.007]

30. **Peck, J., & Shu, S. (2009)**: *The Effect of Touch on Perceived Ownership*

Demonstrates how warm-touch materials like leather and wood influence trust. [Journal of Consumer Psychology, DOI: 10.1016/j.jcps.2008.04.004]

31. **Architectural Digest (2021)**: *LVMH Paris HQ Tour*

Case study showcasing luxury through restraint, tactility, and minimalism. [Source: www.architecturaldigest.com]

32. **Bloomberg (2017)**: *Bloomberg HQ Sustainability Report*

Overview of the $1.3B sustainable, luxurious workplace by Foster + Partners. [Source: www.bloomberg.com]

33. **Dezeen (2022)**: *Roche Diagnostics Office Tour*

Features Scandinavian-inspired luxury in a healthcare setting, balancing warmth and function.

[Source: www.dezeen.com]

34. **Workplace Insight (2023)**: *Accenture Innovation Hub, Milan*

Discusses high-touch, modular design that merges luxury with immersive tech. [Source: www.workplaceinsight.net]

35. **Norman, Donald (2004)**: *The Design of Everyday Things*

Introduces the aesthetic–usability effect and warns against overdesign. [ISBN: 978-0465050659]

36. **Vorecol (2021)**: *Collaborative Workspaces & Innovation*

A research-focused platform covering how collaborative environments enhance creativity and productivity.

[Source: www.vorecol.com]

37. **Gallup (2020)**: *State of the American Workplace Report*

Emphasizes the role of in-person interaction in fostering trust and alignment. [Source: www.gallup.com]

38. **Wired (2015)**: *The Real Value of In-Person Collaboration*

Commentary on how face-to-face collaboration ignites creativity and workplace culture.

[Source: www.wired.com]

39. **Spacepool & Jostle Blog (2023)**: *Designing for Networked Teams*

Insights into open-plan layouts and the ROI of collaborative visibility. [Sources: blog. jostle.me, www.spacepool.com]

40. **TechReport (2022)**: *The Productivity Metrics Behind Open Offices*

Statistical analysis comparing communication and productivity in different office formats.

[Source: www.techreport.com]

41. **Clockify (2023)**: *Noise & Productivity in the Workplace*

Reports on distraction time, email overuse, and the hybrid advantage in open offices. [Source: www.clockify.me]

42. **Glamour (2021)**: *Office Noise & Emotional Well-being*

A review of how acoustics affect mood and output in workspaces. [Source: www.glamour.com]

43. **Environmental Psychology Meta-Analysis (2023)**: *Hybrid Office Satisfaction Study*

Published findings on how mixed-layout offices improve well-being and reduce turnover. [Source: arxiv.org]

44. **Adobe Business Blog (2023)**: *Productivity in Private Workspaces*

Quantifies distraction time reduction in well-designed private pods. [Source: business.adobe.com]

45. **Rivier University Study (2021)**: *Cognitive Load in Open Environments*

Academic analysis of mental fatigue, stress, and cognitive performance in varying office layouts.

[Source: www.rivier.edu]

46. **Steelcase Innovation Center (2022)**: *Case Study in Diverse Collaboration Spaces*

Office design showcases a balance of movement, privacy, and collaboration. [Source: www.wired.com]

47. **Cisco Studio Labs (2023)**: *Tech-Rich Collaborative Hubs*

Describes adaptive work zones using AR, reconfigurable walls, and smart planning. [Source: www.cisco.com]

48. **Goodreads**: [Source:https://www.goodreads.com/quotes/5934-i-ve-learned-that-people-will-forget-what-you-said-people]

49. **Wikipedia (2024)**: *Activity-Based Working (ABW)*

Describes ABW's principles of layout by activity type, boosting engagement. [Source: en.wikipedia.org]

50. **Frontier Fitouts (2023)**: *Designing Brand-Infused Workspaces*

Highlights methods to embed company values via color, material, and texture.

[Source: www.frontierfitouts.com.au]

51. **Bowen Interiors (2023)**- *Design That Reflects Company Culture*

Case-based insights on furniture layout, lighting, and cultural storytelling through space.

[Source: www.boweninteriors.com.au]\

52. **FMGI (2022)**- *Mission-Led Workspace Design*
Overview of physical branding strategies rooted in identity and values. [Source: www.fmgi.com]

53. **Medium (2023)**- *Color Psychology in Office Branding*
Describes how specific colors influence emotional perception and behavior in branded environments.
[Source: www.medium.com]

54. **Architectural Digest (2024)**- *Saie Beauty HQ and Brand-Informed Interiors*
Features a sustainable design that integrates corporate identity through material and color.
[Source: www.architecturaldigest.com]

55. **OH! Design Studio (2023)**- *Environmental Graphics as Culture Tools*
Case study: Dura Roof's integration of corporate messages through signage and wayfinding.
[Source: www.ohdesignstudio.com]

56. **The Dreamr Project (2023)**- *Office Identity in Global Rollouts*
Study on how Criteo balances local culture and global brand consistency.
[Source: www.thedreamrproject.com]

57. **K2Space (2023)**- *Criteo's Multi-City Design Approach*
Breakdown of how branded touchpoints vary across regions while maintaining visual language.
[Source: www.k2space.co.uk]

58. **Studio AsA (2023)**- *Designing for All Five Senses*
Research-backed take on scent, sound, and tactile branding in office spaces. [Source: www.medium.com]

59. **O+A Studio (2023)**- *Analog Spaces in Digital Companies*

Discusses Facebook's Analog Lab, Yelp's War Room, and the power of tactile design in tech.

[Source: www.newyorker.com]

60. **TSK Group (2023)**- *frog Design's HQ as a Brand Manifesto*

Case study showing how heritage and brand storytelling come alive in spatial design. [Source: www.tskgroup.co.uk]

61. **Wikipedia (2024)**- *Visual Brand Language Theory*

Describes how form, color, and material contribute to immediate brand recognition. [Source: en.wikipedia.org]

62. **Deskbird (2023)**- *Task-Based Zoning & Workplace Productivity*

Research showing how physical flow zones reduce cognitive friction and interruptions. [Source: www.deskbird.com]

63. **Glamour (2021)**- *Who You Sit Next To Impacts Output*

Reports productivity increase based on Harvard & Cornerstone pairing studies. [Source: www.glamour.com]

64. **Wired (2022)**- *Hot-Desking Chaos in Modern Offices*

Analysis of time waste, tension, and low morale in unregulated desk systems. [Source: www.wired.com]

65. **Deskflex Blog (2022)**- *Ergonomic Furniture and Employee Health*

Survey highlighting discomfort and absenteeism due to poor seating. [Source: blog.deskflex.com]

66. **Psicosmart (2023)**- *The Role of Ergonomics in Cognitive Wellness*

Research on the correlation between physical discomfort and mental focus. [Source: www.psicosmart.net]

67. **University of Calgary Study (2021)**- *Micro-Stressors in Office Environments*
Identifies overlooked stress contributors like lighting and noise as productivity disruptors.
[Source: blog.deskflex.com]

68. **Ace Office Systems (2023)**- *Natural Light's Cognitive Benefits*
Cites uplift in performance and reduction in physical symptoms with daylight use.
[Source: www.aceofficesystems.com]

69. **Wikipedia (2024)**- *Light Ergonomics*
Covers glare, contrast, and flicker as key contributors to eye strain and reduced focus. [Source: en.wikipedia.org]

70. **The New Yorker (2023)**- *Why Open Offices Fail Productivity*
Investigates stress, illness, and lowered attention spans in exposed environments.
[Source: www.newyorker.com]

71. **arXiv (2023)**- *Cognitive Load and Multi-Talker Environments*
Peer-reviewed study on distraction levels and performance dips in noisy spaces. [Source: arxiv.org]

72. **Steelcase Global Survey (2020)**- *The Power of Quiet Zones*
Survey: 85% of employees need silence to do focused work effectively. [Source: www.steelcase.com]

73. **arXiv (2023)**- *Material Acoustics in Shared Spaces*
Documents how materials like carpet and ceiling tiles improve decibel levels and calm. [Source: arxiv.org]

74. **WELL + ASHRAE (2023)**- *Ventilation and Indoor Air Quality Standards*
Indicates a 19% decrease in illness and 1% rise in cognition with improved airflow. [Source: www.psicosmart.net]

75. **Viscong (2023)**- *Biophilic Design Boosts Productivity*
Shows a **15%** uplift in output with the use of greenery and natural textures. [Source: www.viscong.com]

76. **TIME (2021)**- *Plants and Mental Clarity in the Workplace*
Explains how visual greenery reduces stress and restores concentration. [Source: www.time.com]

77. **NY Post (2024)**- *The Power of Workspace Setups*
83% of organized workers report increased daily productivity through intentional design.
[Source: www.nypost.com]

78. **Haiken Design (2023)**- *Top Office Design Mistakes Businesses Make*
Lists costly errors like over-styling and ignoring acoustics.
[Source: www.haikendesign.com]

79. **Uniworks Designs (2023)**- *Why Employee Input Matters in Office Planning*
Emphasizes real-user feedback in avoiding layout failures.
[Source: www.uniworksdesign.com]

80. **JLL (2024)**- *Future of Work Survey*
Data-driven design practices that evolve with hybrid, tech-forward needs. [Source: www.jll.com]

81. **WELL Building Standard (2024)**- *Indoor Environmental Quality Guide*
Outlines standards for air, thermal, and noise comfort for wellness-led design. [Source: www.wellcertified.com]

82. **WeWork (2024)**- *Hybrid Work Environment Survey Report*
Insights into space agility, tech integration, and evolving workstyles. [Source: www.wework.com]

83. **Architectural Digest (2024)**- *Modern Office Design Trends*
Covers integration of functionality, sustainability, and inclusivity in interiors.
[Source: www.architecturaldigest.com]

84. **Wired (2022)**- *The Efficiency Trap in Over-Engineered Workspaces*
Explores how high-style, low-utility offices harm performance. [Source: www.wired.com]

85. **Courier Mail (2023)**- *What Gen Z Wants in Office Spaces*
Gen Z's need for flexibility, wellness, and personal expression in design. [Source: www.couriermail.com.au]

86. **Financial Times (2023)**- *The Rise of Office Pods*
Reviews the ROI on private acoustic pods and micro zones.
[Source: www.ft.com]

87. **Spotify Design (2023)**- *Designing for Focus and Flow*
Showcases a balance between creativity, mental health, and spatial layout. [Source: www.spotify.design]

88. **IWMS Analytics Reports (2023–2024)**- *Workspace Intelligence Dashboards*
Workplace data used for optimizing spatial planning and resource use. [Source: www.iwmsanalytics.com]

89. **Allen, J. G., & MacNaughton, P. (2017)**. *The impact of lighting on human health and performance in the built environment: A review*. Harvard T.H. Chan School of Public Health. [Source: https://forhealth.org]

90. **LEED Certification Standards Manual (2024)**- *Sustainability Guidelines for Offices*
Green building benchmarks that contribute to cost-saving and environmental compliance.
[Source: www.usgbc.org]

91. **Harvard Business Review (2017)**- *The Power of First Impressions*

Explores how people form lasting judgments within milliseconds during professional encounters.

[Source: https://hbr.org/2017/07/the-power-of-first-impressions]

92. **Gensler Workplace Survey (2023)**- *Designing for Innovation and Engagement*

Reveals that employees in well-designed offices are 2x more innovative and **31%** more productive.

[Source: www.gensler.com]

93. **Deloitte Real Estate Trends Report (2022)**- *Adaptive Use & Brand Alignment in Investments*

Research on how investors assess workplace design for future-readiness and risk signals.

[Source: www2.deloitte.com]

94. **KPMG Ignition Centers (2020)**- *Experience by Design*

Case study on how stakeholder-focused space design drives decision-making and innovation.

[Source: advisory.kpmg.us]

95. **Atlassian HQ Sydney (2022)**- *Tech-Driven Design for Stakeholder Satisfaction*

Features a user-first design that supports client visits, employee collaboration, and investor tours.

[Source: officesnapshots.com]

96. **LinkedIn Sunnyvale Campus (2021)**- *Purpose-Led Design for Culture and Transparency*

Blends brand storytelling, space flexibility, and wellness-driven zones in one HQ. [Source: www.dezeen.com]

97. **USGBC (2024)**- *LEED Certification Guidelines*

A sustainability framework that contributes to trust signals for investors and wellness for teams.

[Source: www.usgbc.org]

98. **Fitwel Certification (2024)**- *Building Wellness with Measurable ROI*

Describes Fitwel's approach to health-focused spaces, now a key stakeholder benchmark.

[Source: www.fitwel.org]

99. **Architectural Digest (2023)**- *Future of Work Design Guide*

Covers modular design, hybrid integration, and human-centric aesthetics for workplace futures.

[Source: www.architecturaldigest.com]